Index Tracking:

Essential Guide to Trailing Man and Beast

AMETHYST MOON
PUBLISHING

Index Tracking: Essential Guide to Trailing Man and Beast
by Freddy Osuna with Jon Boyd

An Amethyst Moon Book
Published by Amethyst Moon Publishing
P.O. Box 87885
Tucson, AZ 85754
www.ampubbooks.com

Available in these formats:
Paperback ISBN 978-1-935354-88-8 / 1-935354-88-4
eBook (epub) ISBN 978-1-935354-96-3 / 1-935354-96-5
eBook (mobi) ISBN 978-1-935354-97-0 / 1-935354-97-3

Library of Congress Control Number: 2012902624

Dedication

Dedicated to Octavio Pain, Carmen Pain, and my wonderful family—Amanda Lynn Osuna, Gabriel G. Osuna, Abel J. Osuna, and Baby Osuna—who have all played a large part in helping me to find this trail that has led to a blessed life.

INDEX TRACKING
Essential Guide to Trailing Man and Beast

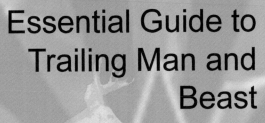

Freddy Osuna
with
Jon Boyd

Contents

Foreword

The information I want to share in this book has been developed for the benefit of both professional and amateur trackers. In 2008 I was honorably discharged from the Marines and hired as a combat tracking instructor at Ft. Huachuca, Arizona. I felt blessed and lucky to not only be paid for teaching tracking, but to contribute to the mission of our armed forces. My work with soldiers, sailors, airmen, and Marines took me to every corner of our country on mobile training teams. The program we taught was developed by the staff of the Tactical Tracking Operations School. Our focus was to enhance the capabilities of military ground operators by providing them with a skill set for visual tracking and ground sign awareness. This two-week program taught team tracking tactics.

It is quite possible the importance of a soldier learning how to track is overshadowed by the byproducts that come about because of learning how to track. For instance, tracking is a tool that although highly dependent on visual acuity, demands all the attributes that commonly make a good soldier. Along with these attributes it requires a change in the way we think as military or tactical operators. In order to be successful at tracking, we must take a critical look at ourselves and be realistic about our own capabilities. The best trackers I have ever taught were the more experienced individuals. They harbored no romanticism of what it was like to be in combat. Their focus was to train and learn as much as they could before they went back to the sandbox. The benefits they saw were enhanced tactical awareness brought on by the ability to identify and interpret ground sign and an increase in sensory awareness, for tracking is only accomplished by integrating all human senses into the task.

Tracking encourages critical thinking. Its success is determined by our ability to problem solve and think objectively. Tracking enhances the security of any ground unit by not only encouraging advanced observation techniques but by creating soldiers who are sensitive to environmental anomalies. These benefits greatly increase survivability in combat.

This is what we strived to give our students at the Ft. Huachuca Combat Trackers Course. It was the subject of many conversations when attempting to advocate for the continuation of a U.S. military Combat

Tracking School. Perhaps these were the only reasons why the U.S. Army stood up the school in the first place. For over two years I taught tracking to the best of my ability because I was focused on developing the tracking skills in each individual going through the course. I found the byproducts I speak of are not obtained or applied well by soldiers trained in a tracking team setting. They can only be taught and apply to the individual human "sensor." It is the collective effort of individually-trained, proficient trackers that can then maximize these capabilities.

My work at the Combat Trackers Course left me wondering, *What if I could change that program to what I felt it should be?* The team-oriented tracking techniques were extremely valuable to employing tactical tracking teams, but we were missing something. We neglected to provide a fundamentals-based foundation in our students and sent them off to hit the ground running with these sexy tactical tracking team tactics. Not only that, we also told them it was the best training they could receive. Why? Because we didn't know better. Well now I know better, and because you opened this book, so will you.

The following information is drawn from my years as a professional combat tracking instructor combined with my experiences as a Marine, and the love of tracking instilled in me as a boy. Most of these techniques are not from my own mind but from lessons learned and witnessed in some cold forest or hot desert, discussed over a Nalgene® of stale water and an MRE. These lessons come from your servicemen, who I humbly submit are some of the greatest trackers in history.

Tracking is a planted seed that when nurtured with knowledge and experience grows and branches out to produce the fruit of situational/ tactical awareness, critical thought processes, enhanced observation, environmental sensitivity, and increased survivability. —Freddy Osuna, USMC Scout Sniper/Tracker

Introduction

Tracking is alive and well in America. Today's trackers are everyday people like you and me, from recreational trackers who practice this trade for fun on their off time, to the professional trackers of law enforcement and the military. There are people out there who have opened their eyes to what many people consider a lost art. It is also an American tradition. In the early years of our great country, field craft played a vital role in everyday survival. Tracking was just one of the many skills people learned as children that forged our national identity. If you read a book about early Americans such as Daniel Boone, Robert Rogers, or Lewis and Clark, you will find that although they came from different eras, tracking played an important part in the lives of many American frontiersmen.

Major Robert Rogers   *Lewis and Clark (with Sacagawea)*

Some of the oldest forms of tracking come from ancient, hunter-gatherer cultures, such as the Bushmen of the Kalahari Desert or the Aborigines of Australia. Their culture and craft is tens of thousands of years old, and they got that way by being very attuned to their environment for the presence of food or danger. The Bushmen, especially, hunt with poisoned arrows, but the poison can take days to work. They must be able to not only track but also identify the individual who is wounded, no matter where they went or how many other members of its herd it mixed with.

Photo courtesy of Ian Beatty

Australian Aborigine   *Kalahari Bushman*

Tracking is also a form of recreation. The majority of American trackers are recreational trackers—just ordinary citizens who at one point in their life fell under the spell of tracking. Some might even call it a curse because it can be so addictive. In either case, recreational trackers are interested in tracking for many reasons, but most of all to have fun in the wilderness and read the signs of creatures in the wild. There are many resources for the recreational tracker to learn how tracking can enhance their outdoor experience.

A short list of tracking resources:

• *Animal Tracks: An Introduction to the Tracks & Signs of Familiar North American Species*. A pocket naturalist guide by Waterford Press

• *Animal Tracks*. A Roger Troy Peterson field guide

• *A Field Guide to Mammal Tracking in North America* by James Halfpenny

- *Tracks and Trailcraft* by Ellsworth Jaeger
- *The Science and Art of Tracking* by Tom Brown Jr.
- *Field Guide to Tracking Animals in Snow* by Louise R. Forrest
- *Scats and Tracks of the Desert Southwest* by James Halfpenny
- *Tactical Tracking Operations* by David Scott-Donelan
- *Tracking: A Blueprint for Learning How* by Jack Kearney
- *The SAS Guide to Tracking* by Bob Carss
- *Tracking—Signs of Man, Signs of Hope: A Systematic Approach to the Art and Science of Tracking Humans* by David Diaz
- *Mammal Tracks and Sign: A Guide to North American Species* by Mark Elbroch
- *Foundations for Awareness, Sign Cutting, and Tracking* by Rob Spieden

Those who hunt can also benefit from knowledge of tracking. Whether a professional guide or a hunter, tracking traces its origins to the hunting of animals for food, clothing, and tools. Most hunters with a little experience are aware of the importance in reading ground sign. With experience a hunter gets better and better at it. With training and experience, he can become downright deadly at it.

In another vein, the application of tracking in law enforcement operations can be traced to Edmond Locard, the director of the very first crime laboratory located in Lyon, France, in 1910. Today's crime scene investigator collects footwear and tire print impression evidence in an attempt to link these objects to individuals and locations. Police officers can apply tracking skills in a wide range of tasks from burglaries to the apprehension of fleeing suspects to search and rescue efforts. Police officers are often trained in basic tracking techniques.

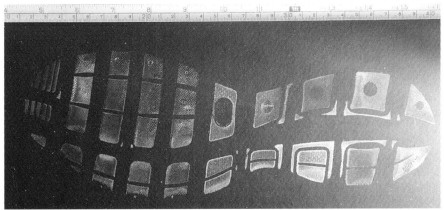

Then there are military trackers. Man has been at war as long as there has been competition for resources and competition between ideologies. The same necessity that led man from footprint to footprint in order to capture or kill his food also contributed to his ability to capture or kill his enemy. The Colonial militias hired Native Americans as scouts because of their tracking abilities, as did the U.S. Army. They eventually created the United States Scouts, a formal unit of enlisted American Indians used to track renegade Apache warriors. In WWII, American and British Soldiers used tracking in an effort to dissuade the Japanese from reaching Australia through the Malayan peninsula. From the combat trackers of Vietnam, Operation Iraqi Freedom, and Operation Enduring Freedom, tracking will remain a basic skill of our American Warriors that has been handed down from generation to generation.

Apache Scouts in the 19th Century

All these thoughts boil down to a couple of universal concepts. First, tracking is tracking, whether you are doing it with animals, humans, vehicles, or whatever. The locomotion is slightly different in each case, but the mechanics are the same. Tracking should have some end result, which is you eventually catch up to your quarry or you have collected the minimal amount of information pertinent to your tracking task. That brings up the concept of transition or contact. Knowing when you are getting close to your quarry and what will/might happen when you catch up is a critical aspect of tracking and one most teachers have left out of their programs.

This is where my system of Index Tracking comes in. As a Native American who has used tracking while growing up as a kid, as a Marine in combat, a hunter, and a tracking teacher, I have become familiar with many different tracking systems and combined the most useful techniques for my own use. This system provides tested, quantifiable techniques for trackers at any skill level, and addresses topics such as search methods, use of Index gates, and transition to contact with the quarry.

So, tracking is a skill that is part of our inheritance as humans. We can all do it, and we can all use the skill in many different ways. It may be of more use in its classical form to the outdoorsman, the military, and law enforcement, but it is not strictly their preserve. It is open to anyone who wants to be more observant and aware of what is going on in his or her environment and wants a fuller experience of that environment. So, if you think tracking and the observation skills it requires may not be for you, think again.

Mammal Mechanics & Mechanical Components

Mammal Mechanics

The study of tracking must begin with an understanding of how the creatures we wish to track move upon the Earth. It is not enough to be familiar with the way a deer moves if that is what I wish to trail. I must understand how all animals move that inhabit the same environment. This is because you will frequently come upon the tracks of other creatures, and if you cannot understand how they are moving in relation to your prey, you will find that these tracks can throw you off of your trail.

The other reason we need to know how things move is because this will give us a frame of reference on where we should look for the next indicator. That's where mechanical components come in. Mechanical Components are the identifiable characteristics of locomotion unique to each animal. First, there are three basic types of locomotion for all land mammals:

The 3 Types of Locomotion

- Plantigrade
- Digitigrade
- Ungulate

Plantigrade (Bipedal): Walking on the soles of the feet, including setting the heel down first.

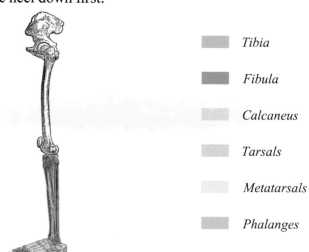

Tibia

Fibula

Calcaneus

Tarsals

Metatarsals

Phalanges

Digitigrades (Quadrupedal): Walking on the front of the feet, setting the ball and toes down first.

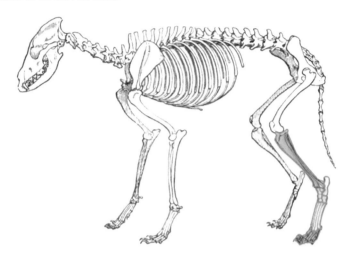

Ungulates (Ungulate quadrupedal): Walking on the toes only.

These three major types of locomotion produce three basic types of tracks. These include:

<u>Plantigrade, Human/Bipedal</u>—Heel strike, Instep, Ball, Toe Dig

<u>Plantigrade, Quadrupedal</u>

Black bear (plantigrade quadruped) in loose dirt. Photo copyright ©Kim Cabrera. Reprinted by permission.

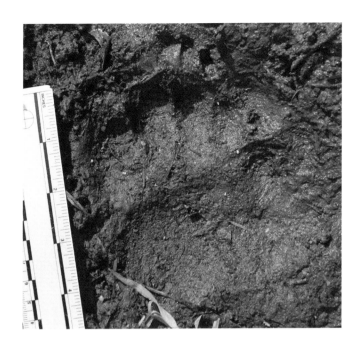

*Black bear print
in mud.
Photo copyright
©Kim Cabrera.
Reprinted by
permission.*

<u>Digitigrade, Quadrupedal</u>—Toe Pad, Inter-digital Pads, Proximal Pads (metacarpal–front/metatarsal-rear)

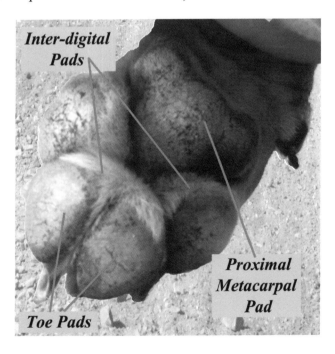

Inter-digital Pads

Proximal Metacarpal Pad

Toe Pads

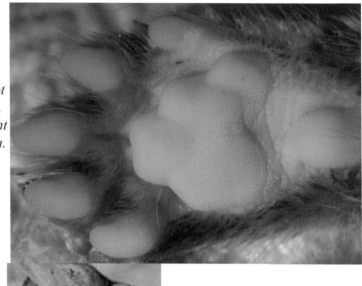

*Right front foot
of ringtail cat.
Photo copyright
©Kim Cabrera.
Reprinted by
permission.*

Ringtail cat

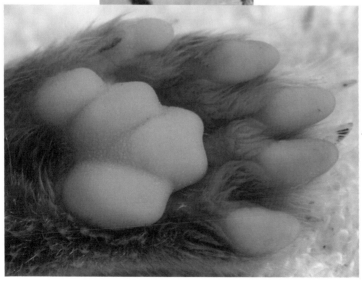

*Left hind foot
of ringtail cat.
Photo copyright
©Kim Cabrera.
Reprinted by
permission.*

<u>Digitigrade, Ungulate/Quadrupedal</u>—Wall, Sole, Pad, Dew Claw

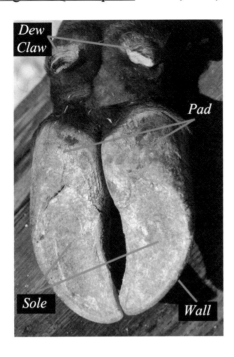

Deer (buck)
with dew
claws showing
Photo copyright
©Kim Cabrera.
Reprinted by
permission.

Deer and bobcat tracks. Note layering of deer on top of bobcat indicating the deer left the track after (on top of) the bobcat print. Also, note direct register of the fore and hind feet in the deer track. Photo copyright ©Kim Cabrera. Reprinted by permission.

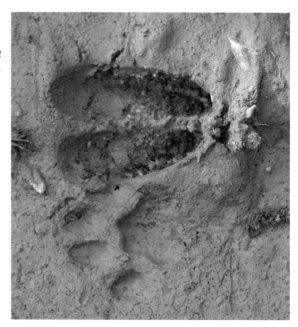

As an animal travels across the ground it leaves a trail or set of tracks. The different aspects of how tracks combine to leave a trail can tell us a lot about the individual who left them, such as their direction, speed, gait, alertness, and specific identity. Gait is defined as:

1. a manner of walking or moving on foot 2. a sequence of foot movements (as a walk, trot, pace, or canter) by which a horse or a dog moves forward [Author's note: or any other creature] *3. a manner or rate of movement or progress* —Merriam-Webster.com/dictionary

Mechanical Components

Locating tracks begins with the study of what we are looking for. These are indicators that living creatures leave behind as evidence of their passage, specifically humans. To find these indicators we must have an idea of where to look. This is where mechanical components come in. Mechanical components are the identifiable characteristics of locomotion unique to each being. There are six mechanical components, which include the four dynamics of a track.

The six mechanical components are: stride, step, pitch, straddle, weight, and pressure. These are used by a tracker specifically to determine what the prey was doing at the scene or along the trail. Although there may be many reasons why a tracker needs this information, the process of looking for these components is standard.

Stride

Stride is the distance between two successive placements of the same foot, consisting of two step lengths. This is measured right-to-right or left-to-left.

Stride

The average stride of a human is 60 inches. As explained by the definition, stride is measured like-to-like, left-to-left, or right-to-right. It is not likely that you will get the same number every time you measure the stride because there are many variables that affect this measurement. An example of these variables is the terrain itself. It may slope, the soil composition might vary frequently, or the prey may have to do a lot of small direction changes to avoid obstacles. To determine the stride measurement, calculate the average by totaling the measurements and dividing by the number of samples you've taken. Averaging is used for all pertinent measurements collected by a tracker. By collecting a series of measurements on a trail, the tracker uses the average number to calculate what activity is taking place at that point on the trail. A tracker is constantly comparing these measurements to those of a being of comparable size and who is moving at an average speed for that specific environment/terrain.

By determining the length of stride the tracker can calculate how fast the prey is moving and therefore determine how much ground he has covered, thereby giving an estimation of his current location. Stride also gives the tracker an idea of the prey's current level of energy. If the stride is slowly decreasing in length and his overall mechanical components appear to be growing more sluggish, you can deduce that your prey is becoming fatigued. Stride can also show what's called "loading up." This is seen three or four steps before a major direction change. This only applies to a being that is consciously navigating terrain as opposed to one who is suffering a mental deficiency. As we move, our direction changes are gradual. As we come to a point where we need to pivot to change our heading we will take shorter steps in an effort to maintain our center of balance and redirect our momentum. This causes shorter strides just before a turn. Reading this can help you to anticipate a coming change of direction. A common myth about stride is that you can determine if the prey is left- or right-handed. The idea is that the dominant leg will be stronger, therefore showing a longer stride. I have tried to prove this theory many times in men and women; however, the results have always proved to be inconsistent.

Step

Step is the distance between the placement of one foot and the following opposite foot.

The step component is used for the same purposes as the stride. The step of an average adult human averages 30 inches and will actually range from 24 to 36 inches. I will often use step to determine speed, direction, fatigue level, and location of the prey because I am more likely to find a step than a stride on a trail because of its size. With Index Tracking we do more with less so this is my preferred method of obtaining this information. I also prefer this method because the length of step is directly proportional to a quadruped animal's length from shoulder to hips in a normal walk.

Pitch

Pitch is the angle the feet point in relation to the prey's centerline of travel. The pitch angle can be measured as positive, neutral, or negative. Another way of measuring this is with a protractor, which is a common method used by wildlife biologists. This method will give you an exact angle measured in degrees. Our preferred method will be the former one. The reason is you will have to determine pitch angle constantly while using the Index Tracking method. You are using visualized containment areas of travel, and how you get the left lateral and right lateral ("lat" for short) limits of these areas starts with the prey's pitch angle in relation to his direction of travel.

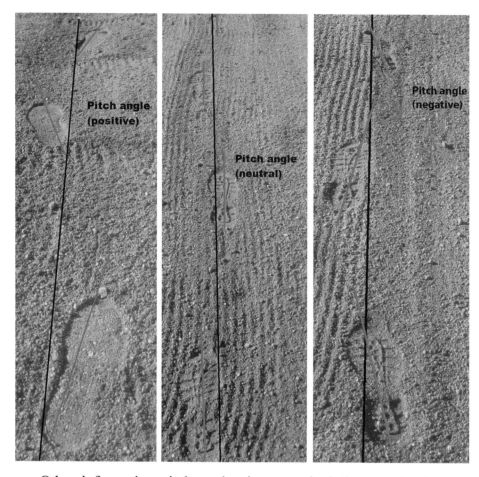

Other information pitch angle gives you includes eye dominance, bearing of weight, injuries, and physical abnormalities, but direction of travel is critical in order to stay on the track.

The key to being able to determine direction of travel relies on your ability to know which way the prey's feet point in relation to his centerline of travel. People do not walk straight lines in the bush, so beginning trackers will find identifying a left foot or a right foot with 100 percent accuracy will be more challenging than they think. So, if you mistakenly identify a left foot as a right foot and your quarry has a strong positive pitch, then the right lateral limit you imagine is actually at your prey's left lateral limit and you are now headed in the wrong direction. You will soon go into spoor search procedures unless you can identify the mistake in time.

Containment area based on
lateral limits for positive pitch

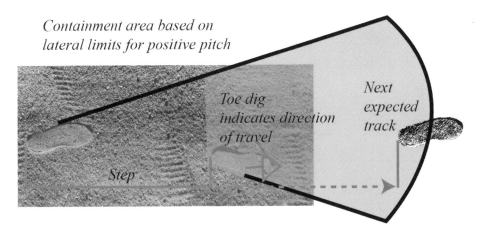

Toe dig
indicates direction
of travel

Step

Next
expected
track

Containment area for neutral pitch   Containment area for negative pitch

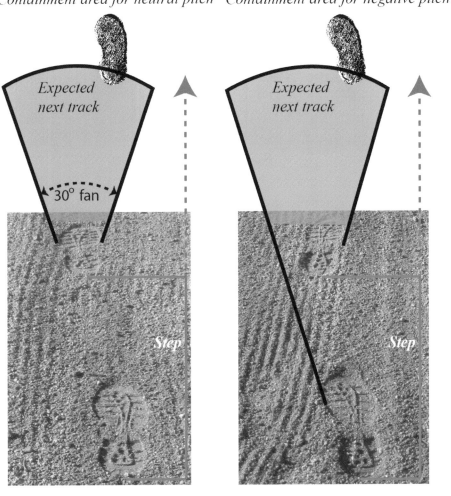

Expected
next track

30° fan

Step

Expected
next track

Step

What if the prey has a negative pitch, meaning his toes point to the inside (pigeon-toed)? The direction is still determined by his baseline pitch in relation to his centerline of travel. What changes are your reference points for what your right and left lateral limits are. The right foot big toe now points to the left lat limit, and the left foot big toe now points to the right lat limit. If the prey has a neutral pitch or the medium is a type in which you really can't determine an angle either way, then I want you to use a 45-degree visualized containment area left to right. If the prey is moving erratically, you can increase the size of that angle, but the main purpose is containment of his spoor within a hypothetical box where you can look for the next track. This method of visualizing a containment area works very well, and if you can anticipate when he might change direction before the trail shows you he has done so, you are experiencing what Index Tracking is all about.

Carrying weight does not affect every person's mechanical components in the same manner, especially in how it affects pitch angle. Some people will compensate for the load by bringing their feet in under their center of gravity, therefore reducing straddle (see photo on page 28) and causing a neutral or negative pitch. Or, some people may widen their stance to create a more stable platform. Ask yourself how it looks while they are moving and while they are standing still. If you experience an abnormality in one mechanical component, it is highly likely that all six will be affected in some way.

Pitch angle can also help you determine eye dominance. Why is this important? It is important for one reason: it helps you to determine his centerline/direction of travel. Two thirds of the population is right eye dominant. Just because a person is right eye dominant does not mean they are right-handed, although the majority of right-handers are, and vice versa for left-handers. The question always arises in human tracking, "If I can tell a person is left handed, then I can narrow down my suspects, right?" I believe the answer is "yes" because only 20% of the world population is left-handed. So if I have ten suspects, it is likely that two of them are left-handed. The problem is that eye and hand dominance are not consistently related. That's why I specify you can figure out eye dominance, not left- or right-hand dominance.

How we do this takes a lot of practice and good tracking conditions. As a person walks they subconsciously search for the horizon in their periphery. This gives them orientation and helps balance their equilibrium. Our eyes are what we use to navigate from one place to another. As we walk or run, our mind chooses reference points to walk toward with the information provided by the dominant eye. The foot associated with the dominant eye points in the direction of travel when a direction change is made. It is during these direction changes the indicator for eye dominance is most visible. You will also see along the trail that the dominant eye side foot is less pitched and more on line with the direction of travel than the non-dominant eye side. The foot points to where you want to go.

When it comes to figuring out if a person is right- or left-handed, you may also use indicators when they are carrying something. If a person is carrying a rifle, he will usually have it on his strong side. When he fires the weapon it will be placed in the strong shoulder. Another good indicator is when a person takes a knee. If a person has a rifle in their hands and takes a knee, nine times out of ten they will place the dominant-side knee on the ground first to rest. After being static for a while they may switch knees because the weight becomes uncomfortable, but by layering the tracks you can sort through and figure out which was down first. You should also look for butt stock impressions on the strong side or scrapes in the dirt from the muzzle of a rifle or other weapon. One note of caution: If a person is right-handed but left eye dominant because of a visual deficiency in the right eye, and they are a professional soldier or shooter, they will commonly train themselves to shoot left-handed so the weapon will be on the dominant eye side rather than the dominant hand side.

Straddle
Straddle is the distance between the furthest points of the outside of the feet or the gap in between the closest parts to the inside of the feet.

Straddle

This gives you information such as approximate width at the shoulders or hips. It is also an indicator of your prey's body makeup, such as do they have a small, medium, or large build? If they are bearing weight, the straddle along with the individual footprints will be an indicator of this, especially a load of over 40 pounds. The heavier the load the more it will affect the prey's baseline measurements.

Generally, extra weight being carried results in a decrease in straddle and pitch

If you believe they have been carrying a load the whole time you've trailed them and, therefore, have not recorded a baseline measurement, then you will need to compare the suspect measurements with those of a person of similar size. This brings us to the subject of weight.

Weight

Weight is used specifically in relation to body composition or the bearing of a load. Why would a tracker need to know the approximate weight of another human or animal? The reasons are many, and here are a few examples. The first is the game hunter; they are looking for a specific type or size of animal, either for meat, trophy, or both. Their ability to recognize differences in the mechanical components as related to an animal's size and weight are crucial in the prioritization of their efforts.

Four-legged creatures carry most of their weight up front. This is because more muscle mass has developed there to support the cantilevering of the head.

The buck's head, neck, and antlers affect weight distribution.

If you are tracking a cloven-hoofed animal, you will find that the fore hooves are larger in surface area than the hind hooves. Also, the depth of the hoof will be deeper in the soil in the fore end. The distribution of weight that is indicated in the animal's feet can also be clue to the hunter what type of trophy it is. An elk displaying splayed or spread toes in the fore end during a natural gate along with abnormal depth is indicative of a large set of antlers. For the man tracker who is tracking a human, weight is significant in developing a profile of the individual being tracked, along with taking note of all the other mechanical components.

For instance, a Marine in Afghanistan will develop a picture in his mind of whom he is tracking. The more information that Marine collects, the more complete this image becomes of his prey. So when that insurgent decides to run to the nearest populated area and attempt to blend in with the civilian population, the Marine tracker may still be able to positively identify that individual through information/intelligence gained along the trail. If an individual is carrying a weapon, the heavier the weapon the more the six components will be affected by the weight distribution of this weapon. I have seen in combat that whenever a patrol stops somewhere, there are weapons marks left on the ground after they get up and step off. At these security halts is where you can focus for indications of weapons and equipment. In some cases the military tracker can tell what type of weapon or weapons the prey is carrying by looking for these indicators.

The key to determining weight of your prey is by having a frame of reference. Animal tracking reference manuals and field guides are crucial even for the most experienced animal tracker.

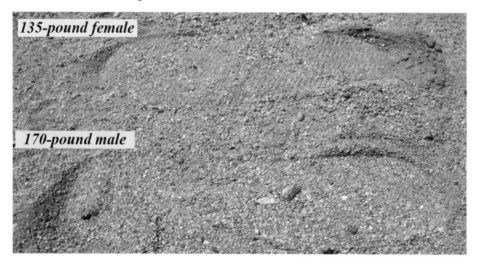

135-pound female

170-pound male

When it comes to tracking humans we can determine approximate weight by a fairly simple method: comparing our own weight to that of the prey. Simply by stepping in the same type of soil in the same type of manner with the same type or similar footwear, we can get an idea of our prey's weight.

I like to bracket the number within 10 to 15 pounds, for example 180 to 195 pounds. The more confident I am, the smaller that bracket becomes, and I will verify this weight estimate along the way. I have seen wooden dowels or rulers used in the comparison, but I have never used this method with success. Weight is going to be indicated in the single track or footprint. We are looking for depth, detail in tread pattern, and the track wall—the outer edge of the track.

Typically the more weight, the more detail there will be in the track. If you stamp a piece of paper with a seal, the more pressure you apply, the better the detail. Consider the type of tread the prey is wearing. If he is wearing deep lugs and cleats, then they may penetrate the soil deeper causing you to overestimate his weight. The track wall is formed by the depth the foot sinks into the tracking medium, but it is also a raising of the soil around the edge of the track caused by displaced soil and air as a body shifts when transferring weight to the next foot. The track wall shoots upward and outward from the center of the foot. The more weight, the more prominent the track wall.

Pressure

Pressure is related to force, momentum, or speed. Your ability to read pressure specifically applies to a single track. Like all other components the tracker needs to be able to read pressure because it plays its own individual role in the prey's story. Pressure gives us a lot of information. The most commonly known use of the indicator of pressure is speed. If the tracker is unable to determine speed because, for example, the ground is too hard or he just cannot find a step or stride, by looking at the toe dig alone and the amount of disturbance and displacement present, the tracker can make a good estimate of how much force it took to cause this. On many occasions I have found that pressure has helped me to confirm or deny whether what I was looking at was my quarry. For instance, a scenario might go like this: A U.S. Army tracking team is on the trail of a man they suspect placed an Improvised Explosive Device (IED). They believe this man to be armed with an AK-47, so their approach is very cautious and deliberate. After an hour of tracking, the team has exhausted their spoor search procedures and is having a hard time picking it back up. The leader of the squad does one last ditch search for the spoor and finds a deep toe dig with a lot of pressure that appears to be moving in the same direction as the prey. The squad leader knows his tracker has walked all over this area in an attempt to re-acquire the spoor, but he also knows how fast he was moving when he did it. With further investigation this knowledge allows him to deduce this is his prey's toe dig and was not caused by his own man.

*Toe dig
left by man
running in
previous photo
sequence.*

If you know the enemy and know yourself, you need not fear the result of a hundred battles. If you know yourself but not the enemy, for every victory gained you will also suffer a defeat. If you know neither the enemy nor yourself, you will succumb in every battle. —Sun Tzu

Terminology

Now that we have introduced some of the basic standard terms used in describing an animal's gait, here is a list of other terms trackers use with each other while practicing their craft:

Ground Spoor - Marks or impressions on the ground that have been made by any part of the body.

Top Spoor - Displaced or damaged vegetation that can be determined to have been caused by the prey.

Hard (Definitive) Spoor - A disturbance in the environment that undeniably belongs to the prey.

Soft (Tentative) Spoor - A disturbance in the environment that could possibly belong to the prey, but requires further evidence.

Bodily Fluids - Any substance that originates from a human or animal orifice, to include waste and blood spoor.

Non-visual Spoor - Those clues that are identified by the human senses other than sight to include subconscious cues.

Byproducts - Examples for different species: owl - pellets, human - litter, deer - sheds, snake - molt

Dwellings - Lays, nests, holes, burrows, dens, shelters, hides

Marks and impressions - Rubs, scent marks, territorial markers, behavioral indicators, tool marks

Anchor Point - Your last definitive spoor. You must always be able to get back to this point.

Relative Age - The estimated age of the track or spoor based on the factors that affect ageing.

Absolute Age - Your final determination on the age based on quantifiable evidence only.

Relative Size - The estimated dimensions of your track based on soil composition and environmental effects.

Absolute Size - Your final determination of the dimensions of the track. This is determined by averaging a series of measurements; no less than three.

Averageing - This method is used in all pertinent measurements used by a tracker by collecting a series of measurements on a trail. The tracker uses the average number to determine the dimensions of a track or spoor.

Search Methods - A system of options used to acquire sign initially or subsequently.

Initial Search - Methods such as sign cutting, range, area, and point searches used to establish a trail.

Point Search - Done in your prey's dwelling or rest area. It is the actual collecting of information. This procedure is done when a specific set of tracks are located. It can be done also at your prey's last known point of origin.

Subsequent Search - Methods such as cross-graining, contour search, long cutting, and wedging used to reestablish a trail or speed up the chase.

Sign Cutting - A method used by a tracker whereby he uses terrain features such as washes or roads to eliminate or confirm the presence of his prey.

Range Search - A preliminary study of the prey's area of occupation. This survey must include the analysis of the four basic necessities: food, water, shelter, security.

Area Search - The observation and study of the prey's immediate dwelling area. Used to gain information as to habits and routines.

Layering - A method of categorizing tracks by the order in which they were placed.

Natural State - The ground or environment undisturbed or unaffected by the prey.

Hot Trail - A trail the prey is likely to be moving on and within reasonable distance of making contact.

Cold Trail - A trail the prey is not likely to be moving on.

Track Trap - An area such as a dirt road, sandy wash, dust patch, or moist ground that leaves definitive spoor when traveled upon by an animal. Useful in sign cutting and search procedures.

Mechanical Components - The identifiable characteristics of locomotion unique to each animal.

Stride - The distance between two successive placements of the same foot, consisting of two step lengths. Measured right-to-right or left-to-left foot.

Step - The distance between the placement of the left and right feet, or right and left feet in quadrupeds.

Pitch - The angle the feet point in relation to the trail or straddle line (positive for outward, negative for inward).

Straddle - The distance between the farthest points of the outside of the feet, or the gap in between the closest parts to the inside of the feet (positive to indicate foot spread, negative to indicate overlap).

Pressure - Indicator specifically related to momentum or speed.

Weight - Indicator specifically related to body composition or the bearing of a load.

Heel strike - The part of the track caused by the placement of the rear part of the foot.

Instep - The part of the track caused by the arch of the foot.

Ball - The part of the track caused (generally) by the widest portion of the foot.

Toe Dig - The part of the track caused by the tip of the foot when it pushes off the ground.

Track Wall - The outer vertical edge of the track.

Wall - The hard outer portion of the hoof.

Sole - The softer material made of carotene (similar to fingernails) contained within the wall of the hoof.

Pad - A weight-bearing material, the pad is an individual characteristic of each species.

Dew Claw - Pads that usually present to the rear of the hoof in ungulates except for antelope.

Plantigrade – Heel-to-toe walking motion characteristic of the human and bear, where the heel normally lands first when taking a step.

Digitigrades - Animals that walk on toes, like canines or felines.

Ungulate - Hoofed, digitigrades animals whose preferred method of locomotion is trotting or galloping.

Head Count - The four methods used to determine how many individual sets of tracks you are tracking.

Direct Count Method - This technique is used to determine the number of prey by identifying characteristics that may be unique to each individual.

Average Pace Method (single stride) - Using the stride of the prey to define the limits of the search area, each full or partial print is counted. This number is divided by the number of feet the prey has. The resulting number is the approximate number of prey in the group.

Comparison Method - This method attempts to replicate the amount of disturbance to the natural state by walking through an area of similar medium multiple times until the desired effect is achieved.

Relative Counting Method - A method used to determine the number of prey by using the baseline measurements of the mechanical components of the prey.

Index Tracking - An advanced method of tracking whereby the trackers are able to determine the location of the next spoor by a precise estimate of direction in relation to the terrain and routines of the prey.

Micro Tracking/Pace-to-Pace - A slow, deliberate, detailed method of tracking used for the collection of information about the prey.

Macro Tracking - An aggressive method of tracking using bold movements in order to close with the prey.

Indicators

The process of tracking is a fundamental-based skill. Like shooting, it requires repetitive practice and repetition of a process or processes. There are three major parts to this learning process: having criteria for what confirmatory spoor is, determining a precise direction of travel, and individual stealth movement/awareness. In order for you to begin learning this trade you must first establish a standard for what you consider to be an indicator of definitive spoor. Take it slowly. If you see a possible or tentative indicator think about the surface area of your quarry's foot. Could it have been done by someone or something else, like other animals or a vehicle? Having a good system of screening definitive spoor will help you to avoid brain blocks and the dreaded yo yo effect.

A brain block happens when you just can't find the next track. That happens most often when the conditions change from what you have become used to seeing when the tracks were made. For example, the quarry may have gone from soft soil to vegetation or onto rocky soil. Right behind having brain blocks, a tracker can end up dwelling on a trail where the transition (and therefore the brain block) took place, causing a stop-and-start condition to following the trail that takes more time and lets the time/distance gap open between the tracker and his quarry. This gap is critical to understand because even though the distance between the tracker and the quarry remains the same, the time gap can vary with many different factors. Such things as tracker capability, the medium the tracks are on, or difficulty of terrain can change how long it might take to catch up to the quarry.

So far, the picture examples in this book have been made under what would be considered "laboratory conditions," and could already be setting you up for a brain block. They were made in a very benign medium such as fine dust, where every detail of the footprint is clearly visible. However, not every track you ever see will look like that. In fact, rarely will you see a track that beautiful in the wild. When you do, consider it a gift. Animals and people go where they need to as part of everyday living, and they normally do not consider the characteristics of the medium they are walking on. That is why we talk about indicators.

Footprints in changing media (mud to gravel)

They are clues left behind by your quarry, which provide evidence of his passage even though he may not leave a laboratory grade track. One of my tracking mentors, a retired police officer named Randy Merriman, taught me this way. I tell my students to imagine opening two files in their mind. The first file is where you will place tracking procedures and techniques. The other file should contain indicators, and no matter how long you live or how many thousands of hours you spend looking at the ground, you will never completely fill this file. The reason for this is there are an almost limitless number of indicators for a quarry's passage. They will change with the area he moves through, the seasons, the weather, and so on. The indicators for the same quarry can be different from location to location, or sometimes even from step to step. The thing the tracker must be prepared to do is notice these changes in condition and notice what the quarry has disturbed as he passed.

This is how it works: a tracker expects that the medium he is visually tracking on will vary in composition and arrangement. What the tracker is consciously searching for are recognizable images on the ground that will keep him/her on the trail. In order for him to project a search image in his mind and attempt to recognize a matching image, he must have a frame of reference on which to draw. That frame of reference is his indicators file, which is as in depth as his training and experience has allowed. Brain blocks occur when you have no search images available in your indicators file for that specific medium. So what do you do now?

The first part of getting past this brain block is to recognize it has occurred. Easier said than done. Even the best trackers are susceptible to this trap. We often will choose the closest matching search image in our mind and attempt to use this as the correct indicator. Even though this might work sometimes it is not a dependable practice.

After you have recognized a brain block has occurred, stop to assess the new medium and attempt to consciously absorb the new indicators that are present by micro tracking. Micro tracking is a system of tracking in which the tracker is attempting to find every footprint. This is often done using a tracking stick. The length of stride and size of the foot are marked on the tracking stick with a rubber band or a marking of sorts. You will place one end of the stick on the rear edge of the last known print and sweep the stick from left to right in a 30-degree fan, with the direction of travel being the center of your arc. If you have estimated the stride correctly, you should be able to find an indicator within two inches of the tip of the tracking stick. After you have found this one indicator you have not completed your task until you can see indicators throughout the rest of the foot. So now you use the foot measurement on the stick as a search reference. As these small indicators begin to reveal themselves remember to consciously give them a descriptive name and place them in that indicators file in your mind. This is how trackers must train and even though it is time consuming and that large track trap to your direct front is calling for you, don't skip these lessons. It is the hard right versus the easy wrong. Don't misunderstand, I know you cannot catch up to anyone by crawling around on all fours and micro tracking, but the better you are at micro tracking the less you will have to do it. This is to be done in training, and after a while a tracking stick can be replaced by your mind's eye. If a physical object is necessary then use your rifle or local vegetation.

If you do this every time you come across a new tracking medium, you will find yourself experiencing less brain blocks and having to go into lost spoor/sign procedures less often. If you as a tracker or a tracking team find yourself using sign cutting techniques every time in order to reacquire a lost trail, consider what you could have learned or how large your indicators file would be by now. You will always go into lost spoor in those mediums unless you stop to figure out why. As my high school football coach use to say, "If you always do what you always did, then you'll always get what ya always got." (Coach Bob Sicilian, Palo Verde High).

Along with the terms we presented in the terminology list, a tracker develops a vocabulary of descriptive terms which he uses to explain and categorize what he sees. A few examples follow.

<u>Regularity</u>: Patterns in a track that repeat themselves, normally seen in footwear.

Displacement: Removal of an object from its original location. Normally indicated by darker, damp soil underneath, or leaving an open impression in its original location.

Socketing: Movement of an object embedded in the ground, where its impression is now larger than the object, showing a "socket."

Outline: The visual cue caused by the outer shape of the quarry's foot.

Blaze: Depression of vegetation such as grass, or wiping of dew off of vegetation by the quarry.

<u>Color change</u>: Different colors of soil or disturbed vegetation (e,g., change in shine, damp vs. dry soil layers, exposed underside of leaves).

<u>Disturbance</u>: Rearrangement of portions of the medium, such as leaves.

Color change (annotated):

Disturbance (annotated):

Transference: Transfer of a medium by the quarry to another medium. This might include things like soil/mud stuck to a shoe that falls off onto snow, or water marks on a stream bank.

Flagging: An aerial disturbance, such as a broken branch, or overturned leaf on a branch above the trail.

Transference (annotated):

Flagging (annotated):

Contrast: Shadow or change in surface shine caused by the presence of a track.

Pressure cracks: Cracks in the surface of the medium (example: dried mud) caused by pressure from the foot.

Contrast (annotated):

Pressure cracks (annotated):

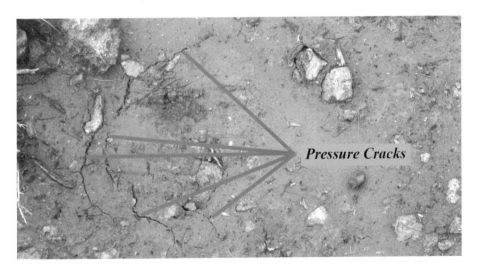

Flattening: An area that has been pressed down in relation to surrounding terrain.

Breaks: Broken twigs, branches, etc. that have been stepped on by the quarry.

Flattening (annotated):

Breaks (annotated):

<u>Scrapes</u>: Caused by the quarry rubbing against a surface, such as a wall or tree trunk while moving. Another example is shown below where animals have scrambled over a wooden fence.

<u>Aerial tension/Cocked vegetation</u>: Displacement of vegetation by the quarry that leaves it set to spring back into its normal position.

Scrapes (annotated):

Aerial tension, same vegetation uncocked:

<u>Browse line</u>: Line formed in vegetation by browsing animals such as deer and goats, where all leaves and sprouts below a certain elevation (normally 5 feet) have been eaten.

Indicators can also be non-visual. For example, certain quarry may leave a smell, such as the musky smell of a javelina in the Southwest. Or, deer and bear have a certain smell (deer remind me of a wet dog, and bear smells like a latrine), especially when you are getting close. You may also hear the quarry moving once you get close, or you may hear other animals' alarm calls as the quarry passes through their territory. Touch may also come into play, as you feel the surface of the medium to test its hardness or feel how dry the sap on a broken branch may be—an important aspect of ageing discussed in the next chapter. Then, there is the "sixth sense." This one is tough to quantify, but it boils down to your gut feel. Someone once explained it to me as a build up of information that your senses are detecting but your brain is filtering out of the picture it presents to your conscious mind. You just get a feeling, and it ends up being right.

Now you can see why I say you will be filling the indicator file for the rest of your life. Next, let's examine the task of telling how long it's been since the quarry passed where you are standing. This is known as ageing.

Ageing

The tracker can only become proficient at ageing spoor by practice and experience. The skill of ageing spoor is a science in itself. Only an experienced tracker can determine the age of spoor with any accuracy. This lesson will give you the basic considerations when attempting to age spoor. Also be aware that tracks age at different rates in different environments, or when conditions change (wet soil drying out in the sun, for instance).

The Greenside Training basic elements of ageing are:
- Surface type
- Weather conditions
- Season
- Moisture in ground/in air
- Vegetation conditions
- Variables (In direct sun light/shaded)

Surface Type

Trackers also refer to this as soil, medium, or substrate. The type of soil you are tracking on in terms of its composition is your first consideration when attempting to age a track. Soil is composed of many different elements. When a living creature moves across the surface, it rearranges the existing state of the soil. The degree of visible disturbance to that natural state will depend on surface type and the amount/type of force applied to it.

Track in dry sand (note sand displacement around the track).

56

Track in moist, shaded sand

Track in mud (marsh environment)

*Track in pine needles
(one of the most difficult media
in which to track)*

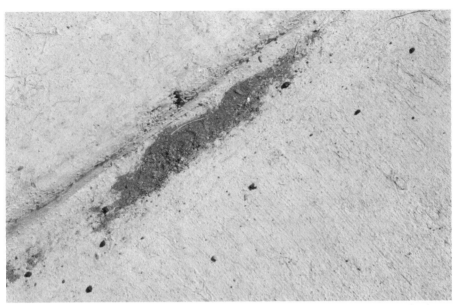

Mini track trap on concrete (note partial tread pattern in the dirt)

Track in silt under water

Tracks on sand and gravel footpath

Weather Conditions

The effects of weather on spoor often serve as an aid in determining the age of a footprint. For instance, if you are hunting deer and you know that it snowed very lightly before daybreak, you can use this fact to determine which tracks are the freshest. The fresh dusting of snow will cover or even fill the tracks that were placed before it snowed. The tracks that happened during or after will be present with either less snow in the tracks or clear imprints on top of the snow. Rain and mist will have similar effects. As experienced outdoorsmen we all monitor the weather forecasts to anticipate what the weather will be like when we are out. As trackers you will need to know what the weather was like in the recent past as well.

Wind is possibly the biggest factor in the ageing process as related to weather. No matter what the geographical location, you can count on the fact air is always moving. When a tracker goes to a new area, he must know what direction the prevailing winds blow from. In Southern Arizona most of our weather comes from the south and will sometimes vary coming from SSE and SSW. This is pretty much a constant year-round. Along with prevailing winds you must be aware of thermal winds.

Warmer air moves to cooler air. In the morning as the sun heats up the air, this air moves upward from low ground to high ground. Later in the evening as the sun is setting and the ground temperature lowers, so does the air, which moves downward from high ground and settles in the low ground. Thermal winds are something to be aware of especially when it comes to scent detection. Prevailing and microclimate winds often render thermal winds unnoticeable.

Season

Most regions have four distinct seasons: fall, winter, spring, and summer, with distinct changes in climate for each season. But other regions on the Earth may have little seasonal change, or may have one of its seasons extended because of its latitude or altitude. For those regions with distinct seasons, each season will present its own unique indicators. If a tracker learned how to track in Anchorage, Alaska, during late August, he will have to approach tracking in January as if he has never been there. This is an extreme example. Most regions will present some indication of seasonal change: animal migration cycles, vegetation change such as leaves dropping, and shift in precipitation levels. Although not so obvious to most people, seasonal changes can provide important clues to a tracker.

Moisture in Ground/Air

Adhesive Quality of Soil

When attempting to age a footprint or determine how long ago the damage on the local vegetation took place, you must consider how much moisture is in the soil and in the air. For example, take a footprint made by the boot of a person moving at an average rate of walking speed. The footprint made by this boot will last a lot longer when it is placed in soils containing more moisture. The reason for this is when you add moisture to soils they assume an adhesive quality. This quality gives it the ability to retain shape for longer periods of time. Think about building a sand castle in wet sand as opposed to dry sand.

Drying Rates of Soil

In addition to understanding the adhesive qualities of soil, you must be able to read the drying rates of moist soil. The distribution of moisture in the soil is not uniform throughout. Generally the deeper you dig, the more moisture you will find. When a person walks, the toe dig pushes back a mound of soil toward the ball. When this happens it reveals the next level of soil that has not been exposed to direct sunlight, heat, wind, and ultraviolet rays. Depending on the composition of the soil and amount of moisture, it will appear darker than the top surface soil. From the moment it is exposed to direct sunlight, heat, wind, and UV rays, it begins to dry out and bleach. The rate at which it dries out can be estimated by the tracker. The best way to do this is by testing and comparing. Walk at the same speed as your prey and compare the color of your toe digs to your prey. The closer you are the darker the toe digs, and the closer your toe digs will match those of your prey.

Moisture and Vegetation

When it should break it bends and when it should bend it breaks. —
Deputy Andy Loza, Pima County Sheriff's tracker

When vegetation is damaged it will attempt to heal itself by clotting, or it will sacrifice that part of itself to save the whole. There is no exact science in determining the healing rate of vegetation. Only your familiarity with the plants in the area in different seasons where you are tracking will build your knowledge base on the subject.

Generally the more moisture in the air, the faster plants will recover. Again this varies by species. Bruising, breaks, tears, contusions, scrapes; often comparing the damage you suspect was left by your prey to a known sample can help to determine its rate of healing. Don't just use your eyes when analyzing the damaged plant. Your sense of smell can be an equally effective tool; the smell of the fresh break will slowly dissipate with time and exposure to the factors that affect ageing.

Variables of Ageing

Variables to ageing are best defined as those factors which present inconsistencies to the effects the elements will have on the deterioration of a given spoor. If your trail is moving along through the flat desert, exposed to direct sunlight and wind, you will find these two elements are affecting your spoor in a consistent manner. When this trail leads into a canyon and suddenly is shielded from direct sunlight and wind by the terrain, it will appear to be significantly fresher than when the trail was in open ground. It is fresher because it is further along the trail but this effect might be deceiving enough to make you believe that you are minutes from contact with your prey. Being aware of these types of variables takes a broad awareness level.

An Ageing Stand

An ageing stand is a controlled experiment a tracker conducts to test elements in his or her environment that may assist in determining the age of spoor. The tracker first gathers material items his prey may utilize and inadvertently leave behind: food scraps, clothing items, items of equipment, and/or waste. The items are placed in an area exposed to the natural elements and conditions to simulate what will be experienced on the trail. The tracker records his initial observations of these items taking note of color, smell, condition, and position. Observations are recorded throughout a 24- to 72-hour period, and data can be compared upon completion of the ageing stand. The same observations are conducted on samples of the local vegetation and sections of trail with footprints on them. Photos, sketches, and even video are useful for parts of the ageing stand. Following are ageing photos of tracks in shade and in sun taken for comparison purposes.

62

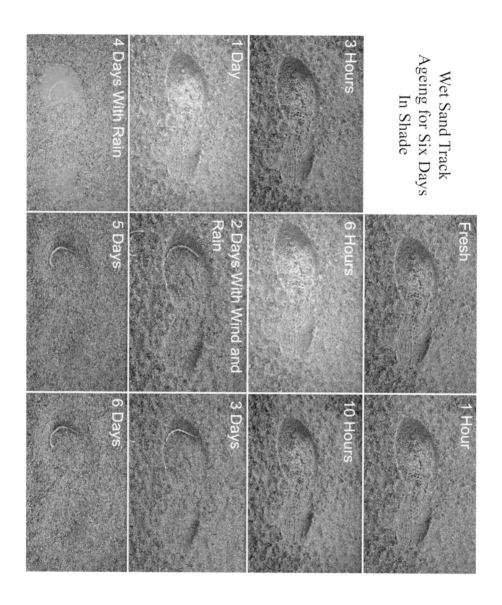

Wet Sand Track
Ageing for Six Days
In Shade

63

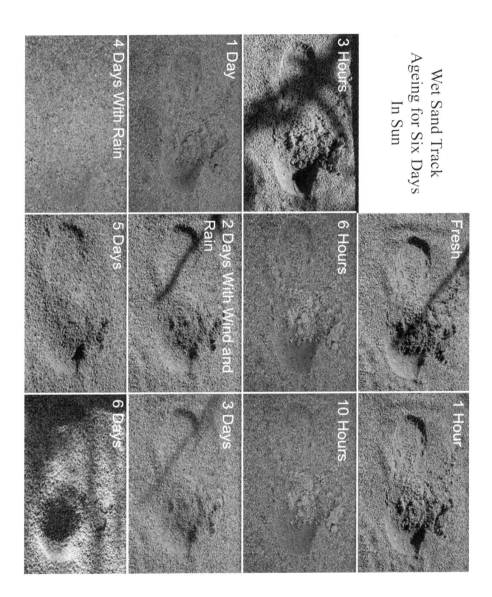

Wet Sand Track
Ageing for Six Days
In Sun

Ground Sign Interpretation

Ground sign interpretation is an essential skill for all tracking professions. It is the process of identifying and interpreting marks and impressions left on the ground in order to recreate the actions that took place in a certain area. There are three main reasons the tracker needs to be able to interpret ground sign, and they are:

• To identify behavioral trends or mental/physical disposition of the prey

• To gain essential elements of information relevant to the tracking task

• To be able to anticipate direction/destination of movement

Interpreting ground sign will give you the tracker's essential elements of information needed to begin trailing your prey. Basically it's a checklist that allows us to assess if this trail is 100% our prey and whether it is worth our time and effort to follow. There are two versions of this checklist, one for human tracking and one for animal tracking.

6 Essential Elements of Information (Human)

• Who - height, weight, profile, I.D., Footwear type
• What - action, activity
• When - date, time, estimated age
• Where - location, estimated destination
• Why - intent, disposition
• How - method of movement

5 Essential Elements of Information (Animal)

• Who - species, dimensions of track, stride, straddle, size, weight
• What - action, activity
• When - date, time, estimated age
• Where - location, estimated destination
• How - gait, method of travel

Procedures and Considerations for Interpreting Ground Sign:

One of the hardest tasks for a tracker is to establish a trail in the first place. The tracker does this by initial search procedures. Once you have conducted your initial search procedures, you may end up completing that process with a point search. The point search can be conducted once an area has been positively identified as having recently been occupied by the prey. A certain identifiable action has taken place at the point search location. A point search location can be a rest area, building exit, feeding area, or watering hole. If your intent is to catch up to the prey from this point then it must be aged and determined to be a hot trail—a trail that the prey is likely to still be moving on and within reasonable distance of making contact with. These will be discussed in greater detail later.

The following is a guideline for attempting to gain as much information on your prey as you can before setting off to track. There are three parts to this process: choosing a start point, collecting the information, and analyzing the information.

Choosing a Start Point

Set yourself up for success. Use your observation skills by glassing from the high ground. Spot and stalk. Find them, and then hunt them.

Know your area. Prep the area by creating drags and monitoring track traps.

Drag on dirt road set up by U.S. Border Patrol

Choose a point. By knowing your prey's habits and routines, you can best anticipate where to find his freshest trail. The point you choose to start from should not be random but an anticipated point you know the prey will visit. Have a list of these marked on your map.

Collecting the Information (Example: Point Search)

Mark a boundary around this area using man made or natural visual markers.

Identify all tracks moving in and out.

When analyzing this area work big to small, gain a general impression before analyzing individual actions.

Age the tracks/impressions using layering. Preceding/Relative/ Residual sign.

Record the mechanical components of each set of tracks.

Collect info on each set of prints, dimensions, sketches, photos, etc.

Analyzing the Information

Analyze the mechanical components, small to big. First look at each print and then work your way through the other components, comparing them to a frame of reference.

Reenact the scene step by step, comparing a known to an unknown.

Once you have collected your essential elements of information and you are satisfied with this information, you will begin the process of tracking.

Confirm this information along the way, and expect it to change.

Examples of Marks and Impressions

Body impressions on the ground: footprints, knee marks, handprints, elbows, butt marks.

Tool marks: weapons, packs, mobility aids.

Animal markings: digs, scrapes, lays rubs, etc.

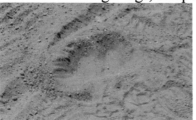

Knee impressions   *Hand prints*

Search Methods

There are two main parts of learning how to track. You have to know what to look for and know where to find it. This lesson deals in the "where to find it" part. In this lesson we will discuss the two types of search procedures used to acquire and maintain a trail.

Spoor Search Methods

Spoor search methods are the procedures that allow you to establish or reestablish the trail. The two methods are initial search methods, such as range, area, and point searches used to establish a trail, and subsequent search methods, such as cross-graining, contour searches, long cutting, and wedging, used to reestablish the trail or to create a short cut.

Initial Search Procedures

- Range Search
- Area Search
- Point Search

Range Search

A range search as described by its definition is nothing more than an analysis of the prey's immediate habitat. It includes the areas where it may forage, hunt, or otherwise acquire all necessary essentials to sustain itself.

There are many social considerations when attempting to identify a human's immediate habitat. Humans are social creatures and with the aid of mechanical and animal transport, we can occupy hundreds of miles of space weekly. It is easier to track the patterns of humans in rural settings than it is in metropolitan areas.

Area Search

The area search is conducted in the area the prey feels most safe. You will find networks of trails leading in and out of this type of area. It is an area the prey will gravitate toward for one reason specifically: it provides concealment, which gives them security. Food and water or resupply will be accessible within a reasonable distance. This will be the human's neighborhood or village. The human's immediate social network is included in this area.

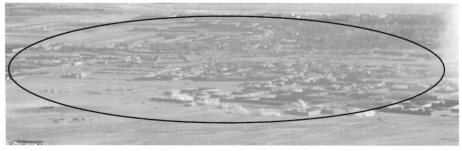

Area Search. Foot trails/canals/defilade/concealed routes and positions. Who is moving in and out and why?

Point Search

A point search is done in your prey's dwelling or rest area. It is the actual collecting of information. This procedure is done when a specific set of tracks are located. It can be done also at your prey's last known point of origin, and that may be confirmed by ageing or by witnesses.

Point Search. Whose tracks are associated with this dwelling? Can you link these individuals to any recent criminal activity or significant events in your area?

These processes are not co-dependent, meaning you don't have to go through each step in order to pick up a trail. What this process allows you to do is to become familiar with the life patterns in your area of operation. By being familiar with the life patterns in your area, you have a bigger picture and are significantly more aware of the activities taking place around you. Who is who in the zoo.

Subsequent Search Methods

- Cross-graining
- Contour search
- Wedging
- Box search
- Crossovers/long cuts/zigzags

Subsequent search methods are the methods used after you've already been trailing your prey. It is a set of options that you can pull out of your toolbox to deal with losing the trail or creating a shortcut.

Cross-graining

Used in conjunction with a known direction of travel—the tracker can use this method to head off the track line ahead in order to cut down the lead gap.

Contour Search

This method is used to reestablish a track by using lines of drift and terrain selection to contain the trail by a process of elimination. This will be your most often used technique in reacquiring spoor. It is done first by moving 15 yards to the rear of the last known point, which is your last definitive (hot) spoor. Then you will sweep out to the left or right at a 90-degree angle depending on which side of the track line you think you are most likely to find it. As you sweep you are going to complete a 360-degree sweep around the last known point, moving from track trap to track trap and covering all gates that the prey might have passed through. It is important to remember that as you are sweeping you are not going to make a perfect circle because you are moving from track trap to track trap. Let the terrain and vegetation be your guide. If you sweep all the way around the last known point without finding the trail, then you must do the process over again, making sure to complete an even wider sweep. Remember not to cross over an area that you have already searched.

A contour search prioritizes your areas of focus. Don't just do a big 360-degree circle hoping to stumble on the tracks.

Wedging

This method is used by identifying the prey's likely paths and eliminating them by physically crossing over them in a wedge shape, also known as cutting the pie. As you do the wedge or cut the pie, first step back from the last known point a couple yards and start off either on the side that you think he is drifting to or the side that provides the best angle of light. If you are sweeping with the sun to your back then you will have a harder time seeing it than if you are moving toward the sun.

Box Search

A systematic search that uses linear features that surround the search area, commonly used in agricultural fields or in a gridded area like an urban environment.

Crossovers/Long Cuts/Zigzags

Methods in which the tracker marks the last known track in case he needs to get back to it and moves forward and cuts across the trail in an attempt to cut down the lead gap. These three methods (crossover, long cuts, and zigzags) accomplish the same goal but are done with different search patterns, which will be determined by the terrain.

Team lead signaling for a crossover (see insets 1 and 2)

These search patterns are very similar to what you use to find that hard-to-find land navigation point or what search and rescue teams use to find missing persons. These are merely guidelines; use your imagination and remember the golden rule:

Either you're tracking or you're conducting a search method. Time in between is lost forever.

Tracking Methods

There are many viable systems of tracking in the world. Many of these systems have been developed throughout history during times of conflict.

In the 1940s the British utilized visual tracking during guerrilla operations against the Japanese. The Japanese were advancing south through the Malayan Peninsula in an attempt at gaining a foothold in order to penetrate the Australian continent. Since then the British have maintained a military jungle tracking and survival program in Brunei. This is where the British 5- and 7-step methods come from.

Ghurkas entering Tokyo at the end of World War II

The British 5-Step Track Pursuit Drill:

- Step 1: Assess general direction of quarry's flight.
- Step 2: Eliminate openings and finalize direction.
- Step 3: Look for the furthest located sign and link back.
- Step 4: Check areas left and right of track line for signs of deception.
- Step 5: Move forward.

The British 7-Step Method:

• Step 1: Assess direction of the quarry, looking as far out as the perceived track line can be seen and back to tracker's position.

• Step 2: Eliminate openings/alternate routes and finalize general direction of travel.

• Step 3: Locate furthest sign and connect it back with certainty to the tracker's position.

• Step 4: Watch for the quarry (concurrently)

• Step 5: Check left and right for anti-tracking measures and attempts at deception.

• Step 6: Tracker plans next movement, identifying where he's going to move and anything in between that might compromise sound discipline, if his steps may contaminate the sign he's following, and obstacles to be negotiated.

• Step 7: Move forward.

In its most fundamental form, this is the first time during the 7 steps the tracker is actually moving. Here the tracker actually moves along the track line, watching for the quarry (flight, ambush, or attempted concealment) until he comes to the previous, furthest point identified in step #1, at which point the cycle begins again.

(7-step method courtesy of David Reeder, put together with assistance of Officer Commanding, British Jungle Warfare Tracking School Brunei via BOLO Report.)

Subsequently, during the Vietnam War in 1966, General Westmoreland ordered the activation of U.S. Army Combat Trackers. These soldiers were sent to the British jungle warfare tracking and survival school where they were certified during a 65-day program taught by New Zealand SAS and British Ghurkas. Combat Tracker Teams used a combination of visual and K-9 tracking to great effect in Vietnam.

75

Photos courtesy of Combat Tracker Teams of the Vietnam War, Inc.

During this same time in the 1960s, the country of Rhodesia was developing a system of tracking specifically to interdict human and weapons trafficking from Mozambique. They turned to a man named Allan Savory, who, along with Rhodesian SAS developed a highly-effective combat tracking method. This system utilized highly mobile tracking teams integrated into a combined arms capability to interdict enemy infiltrators—commonly known as the Rhodesian method.

Photo courtesy of Allan Savory

The Rhodesian Method:

This is a highly aggressive system of visual tracking. This is an advanced method of team tracking that is highly dependent on lost spoor procedures and a system of rules. When using this method it is assumed individual tracking skills have already been achieved.

Rules:

- Identify the correct tracks you wish to follow.
- Mark the start point of the follow-up.
- Never walk on top of spoor.
- Never overshoot the last known spoor.
- When following aerial spoor always seek confirmatory evidence.
- Always know exactly where you are.
- Always keep in visual contact with other team members.
- Always try and anticipate what your quarry will do.

2007 to 2010

U.S. Army Combat Tracking School - This school was conducted at Ft. Huachuca, Arizona, and was the first formal tracker training in the U.S. military since 1970 when the school in Ft. Gordon was closed.

2010 to Present

In October 2010, as a former USMC Sniper and Assistant Task Lead for the U.S. Army Combat Tracking School, I began developing a new system of visual tracking with help from Matthew Moul. We dubbed this new system "Index Tracking," which supplemented the Rhodesian and British methods. The Index Tracking system of training trackers focuses on establishing an individual tracking skill set, which until now has been a capability gap in these systems.

Index Tracking

Index: something that directs attention to some fact, condition, etc.; a guiding principle.

Preparation

Now that you are equipped with a toolbox full of options for acquiring and maintaining a trail, you are ready to begin the art of Index Tracking. As we cover this concept I also want to relate to you where the idea for Index Tracking came from. So bear with a couple of "war stories" along the way.

One of the first and most memorable experiences I had was when I was young. I was around the age of nine when I started to explore the desert. My foster mother, Carmen Pain, was a housesitter for the owners of a place named Tohono Chul Park. This was a 100-acre desert preserve on the edge of North Tucson. This is where my tracking story began.

"Get outside and play," she would say. My brother Ray, who was three years younger than I, was always by my side. We would venture into the desert eager to discover its gifts. After all we had been through in our biological family, we were hungry to enjoy the life of a child. We discovered things through necessity. We created our own shelters when the desert monsoons would come. We hunted for rabbits and small game. We foraged for edible plants. A lot of what we learned we saw on TV, or looked it up in books. We did this for one main purpose: we didn't want to go inside. If we had to go home every time we got hungry or thirsty then that would leave us with less time to play. As far as we were concerned, we had some catching up to do in the "being a kid" department.

These are great memories I have. We taught ourselves to track coyotes, javelina, quail, and small rodents, but never killed them. In fact, we were almost the prey on a few occasions when tracking javelina with small ones. On one occasion I was treed by a sow with piglets. We made primitive spears with some arrowheads we had found at a ruin on the property. We were determined this would be the day we got a pig. We picked up the trail by cutting for sign in the wash behind the house. I would do most of the tracking, and I think Ray would just follow along being a good brother. We trailed a group for about an hour, and when we came upon them, the sow was not happy to see us. As it charged from about 10 meters, I chucked my spear and ran up a mesquite tree. Ray took off towards the house where he listened for my call for help if I needed it, or at least that's what he said he did. Eventually the pigs went away, and I learned a valuable lesson that day about tracking. I had not been ready for what happened when we closed with our quarry. Note to self: adrenaline has a way of indelibly etching life lessons on your psyche.

The first step is to establish a trail using the initial search methods you have been taught. Once you have found the spoor of your prey and have identified it as belonging to your prey, and it is in fact a hot trail, then you are ready to begin. For this lesson we will explain the methods of trailing a human. At our point search we have collected footwear size in inches, sketched the pattern, taken photographs, as well as collected all pertinent information regarding mechanical components.

Always mark the beginning of your trail on your map and on your GPS. Along the way you will continue marking the position of the spoor on your map and on your GPS because it will alert you visually of any movement patterns and trends the prey is making. This allows you to better anticipate his movement.

Body Posture

As you follow the trail the trick is to look out 5 to 15 yards, depending on your visibility, which is determined by the medium, available light, vegetation, and weather. Keep your head tilt upright, as this is the most efficient body posture with regard to fatigue. Plus, the closer your eyes are to the horizon the more likely you are to catch movement in your periphery. This is especially important as you close the gap with your quarry, and your chances of getting a visual sighting increase with a quarry who does not want to be found.

There are many negative effects of tracking too close to your feet, but the two main negative effects are increased eye/body fatigue and loss of situational awareness. Depending on the scenario you could be on spoor for hours or even days. Make sure to have something left when you come into contact with the quarry.

There are three main ingredients of conducting Index Tracking:
• Criteria for definitive spoor/sign
• Determining precise direction
• Tactical awareness and stealth movement

Phase 1: Criteria for Definitive Spoor

In order for beginning trackers to develop a standard for what they should consider to be definitive spoor, they must be given a frame of reference. That is done by the tracker's teacher in the early phases of their tracking training. The criteria for what is to be considered definitive/confirmatory spoor are: 1. Class characteristics (size/shape/pattern of footwear) and 2. Age. *Can I place my quarry at this location within time and space?* Without these two pieces of information you do not have confirmed sign/spoor. With Index Tracking it is not enough just to point out the fact that a rock has been dislodged or a piece of vegetation has been flattened. We must be able to use obvious indicators as a reference point that leads us to the minute details throughout the foot. When added up, they create the image of the foot itself, thereby revealing the evidence of size, shape, pattern, and age.

There are many methods of teaching this, and mine is called a Confirmation Drill. The purpose of the Confirmation Drill is for a teacher to instill or influence the student's standard for what he should consider to be definitive spoor. First the instructor will lay a track line at least 100 hundred yards long. The terrain must be a type that the instructor is very comfortable with but a student would consider semi-difficult (for tracking). The rules are as follows: the student will begin the trail, at first pointing out every left and right foot and three to five indicators in each track. The tracker must verbally explain everything they see to the teacher. The teacher will accept or deny what the tracker says he sees. If he denies something, then the tracker must be able to get him to see it, or he should not have pointed that specific visual indicator out. As the tracker is starting to understand what the teacher's criteria is for definitive spoor, the teacher gives him more and more freedom. This drill works very well in the early stages of learning to track, mainly because it encourages objectivity and analysis. When the tracker is punished for attempting to pass off a halfhearted indicator, then he will search for quantifiable reasoning, resulting in reward. This is the first part of the Index Tracking formula.

Phase 2: Determining Direction

I have shared a lot so far about the basic principles of determining direction of travel or the line of travel by looking at what has been left by the prey. Visualization is an important tool for a tracker. I want you to visualize your prey moving just ahead of you when you trail him. When you do this you will be surprised to find you can determine if that would be a reasonable route choice for the prey or not. Remember, a quarry's behavior can be reflected in his tracks, and most humans will take an easy route versus a more difficult one. If you can determine the direction they are going, you can know where to look for the next track and start to build a pattern of behavior.

To determine direction with only one track I look at two things: the toe dig and which foot I am looking at (left or right). The toe dig gives you a lot of information. It can give you an age, speed, and direction. Direction is determined in the toe dig by finding the long axis of the toe dig, to include the displaced dirt or mound of dirt pushed back. If you draw a line through the long axis of the toe dig with the tip of the apex being the deepest part of the dig, you will have an exact line of travel. Not an approximate line, exact.

Another method I like to use in conjunction with this is the 3-point toe dig technique. I will place three rocks in the toe dig: one to its widest point on the left, one to the widest point on the right, and the third rock will be placed in the apex of the toe dig, or deepest, pointiest part. The shape of the placed rocks forms an arrow that points in the direction your prey went. This is a training aid and like a tracking stick, becomes a tool in your mind's eye. As you get the precise line of travel, visualize that line and look to find the likely gate your prey moved through. When you find that passageway, you must identify a track trap he would have hit if he passed through there. You have now acquired an Index point. Aim small, miss small.

My most serious experience with Index points (I had not come up with a name for it yet) came during the fight for An Najaf in Iraq when my platoon was deployed there. On August 18th, 2004, our unit was two days into the battle for An Najaf at the cemetery, which is supposed to be the second largest in the world. The purpose was to ascertain enemy positions and gather signals intelligence. We took a lot of enemy sniper fire as we pushed forward, and we lost some guys—killed and wounded. We cleared graves and mausoleums. There were underground tunnel systems where the enemy was supposedly hiding in wait. As we would pass by, they would attempt to jump out and shoot us in the back. One of the telltale signs I could see as we moved up were tracks going into the mausoleums, but not coming out. The mausoleum entrances were perfect Index gates. I ran out of grenades quickly as we cleared underground mausoleums. I even used smoke grenades and signal grenades to smoke out anyone hiding underground. After that, using Index gates became part of my routine, and kept me pointed more directly at my quarry.

Phase 3: Stealth Movement

Now that you have acquired an Index point, you need not stumble around looking at the ground depending on others to be on the lookout for your prey or even provide you security. You can now tactically, stealthily move to that Index point. Before you move you will conduct SLLS (Stop, Look, Listen, Smell), being receptive of non-visual indicators—those clues that are identified by the human senses other than sight, to include subconscious cues. Then you will identify the best route to get to that Index point.

I will choose the quietest route in terms of ground foliage if I am hunting. If you are in a hostile environment, you must identify possible danger areas, covered positions along the way, and escape routes. In short, this is the OODA loop cycle as it applies to Index Tracking. *Observe* the information at hand, *Orient* yourself to the environment, and *Decide* your next course of action, *Act* on your decision. Your objective is to shorten the duration of the OODA loop cycle. This is done by training and experience.

Warriors compress time; this is the sixth principle of the art of stalking. Even an instant counts. In a battle for your life, a second is an eternity, an eternity that may decide the outcome. Warriors aim at succeeding, therefore they compress time.
Warriors don't waste an instant. —The Warrior Sayings of Don Juan Matus

As you move to that Index point consider how far ahead your quarry is likely to be. If you think he is within audible distance, you must assume a stalking mode. If you can determine through ageing that he is some distance ahead and imminent contact is not expected, you can move faster from Index point to Index point. In a stalking mode, your route selection to your next Index point is your first consideration. You must choose a route that has cover and concealment, has a means of escape, and is passable. You have to choose the appropriate mode of travel. Are you going to crawl slowly in an attempt to get eyes on your prey? Or are you going to weasel walk in a heel-to-toe, foot-cradling motion. Along with everything else, your mode of travel requires practice. When you arrive at your next Index point, your priority is not to look for a track or at the ground, but rather to observe the terrain ahead for any sign of your prey or any threats to your safety in the immediate area. Once you have visually cleared the immediate area for the presence of your prey or any threats to you, you must scan the area in the distance for the same. Once these two areas are clear, only then are you safe to observe the next spoor and the process starts all over again. Remember: OODA loop.

The Trackers OODA LOOP

The OODA process below is written as if you were following a suspect or enemy, but the process is the same whether trailing man or beast—friendly or not.

OBSERVATION

1. **SLLS** (Stop, Look, Listen, Smell)

    a) Visually clear every covered and concealed position, near and far (5's and 25's).

    b) Listen for unnatural noises, absence of natural noises, or animal/insect alarms.

    c) Smell for foreign or displaced scents.

2. **METTT** (Mission, Enemy, Terrain, Troops, Time/space)

    a) Mission – Passive track interpretation for intelligence purposes. Pursuit operations. Reconnaissance.

    b) Enemy – Most probable course of action (EMPCOA).

    c) Terrain – Key terrain, observation and fields of fire, cover and concealment, obstacles, avenues of approach/escape (KOCOA).

    d) Troops – In direct or in general support. Proximity. Adjacent units.

    e) Time/Space – Age of the tracks. Estimated time and distance gap. Theoretical location of suspects. Theoretical search area.

3. **Track Identification**

    a) Size in dimensions

    b) Type of footwear

    c) Pattern of tread

    d) Age of track (Can you place your suspect there within time and space according to what you see in the track?)

4. **Direction of Travel**

    a) Exploit foot orientation (left or right), straddle line, pitch angle, and toe dig pointers in order to reduce the search area.

    b) Properly reading the mechanical components will produce a visualized containment area.

    c) Locate Index point

    d) Identify Alternative Index points

5. Behavioral Indicators

    a) Interpret mechanical components

    b) Patterns of movement

    c) Target indicators (anything that reveals the presence of your enemy to include spoor)

PERCEPTION - The interpretation of the observed information as it pertains to the task at hand. A hypothesis of how this information can be exploited in the trackers favor.

ORIENTATION

    1. Terrain – How can you exploit the terrain to your advantage?

    2. What would be the best patrol route/angle/formation to approach the next Index point?

    3. Will you move slow or fast (as indicated by track ageing)? (Are you getting so close as to anticipate likely contact or does the track tell you that he is likely 1 hour or more ahead of you.)

    4. EMPCOA in relation to the terrain, weather, fatigue.

    5. Does it appear the suspect is aware of the fact he is being followed (alert/awareness indicators)?

DECIDE

    1. Make a decision:

    a) Is it tactically feasible to continue following?

• You have tactical advantage.

• Ground and environment lend to efficient tracking conditions.

• Trail yields high intelligence value

• Hot Trail

    b) Stop and exploit. Are there behavioral indicators within the mechanical components that could be exploited for actionable intelligence?

    c) Should you return to base? (Go no Go)

• Ground and environment present unfavorable tracking conditions.

• Ground and environment present a tactical advantage in the enemies favor.

• Trail yields low intelligence value.

• Suspect has successfully reached extraction out of the area (cold trail)

ACT

Follow

1. By tactically patrolling to your next Index point. You are clearing every covered and concealed position to your direct front en route. Move (Stop, Look, Listen, Smell). Your focus is to see, hear, or smell the enemy before he sees, hears, or smells you!

2. Only by systematically exploiting each track for information that applies to the tactical situation can you patrol from Index point to Index point.

3. When you have arrived at the next Index point, the process starts over again: SLLS/visually clear near and far sectors for danger (5's & 25's), etc.

Stop and Exploit

1. Establish 360-degree security.
2. Establish a perimeter around the area to be investigated.
3. Identify tracks going in and out. Number/type/direction
4. Record all mechanical components and compare to a known or baseline set.
5. Age the tracks and impressions using layering.
6. Determine the actions.
7. Report/exploit.
8. Continue tracking.

Return to Base

1. A patrol is most vulnerable during the beginning (infiltration) and ending (exfhiltration) of any tactical operation. Maintain security.

2. Consolidate information regarding the tracking operation to this point.
   a) Who – Height, weight, footwear (size/type/pattern), profile
   b) What – Action, activity
   c) When – Date, time, estimated age
   d) Where – Location, estimated destination, direction of travel
   e) Why – Intent, most probable course of action
   f) How – Method of movement / travel

3. You will be that much more prepared the next time they are sighted.

Summary

Tracking is a very dynamic process for which we must use all of our senses to effectively accomplish. The more efficiently a tracker handles the trail, the smoother and safer the tactical movement will be. What determines his degree of efficiency is his experience and time spent mastering the fundamentals.

The fundamentals of tracking are establishing criteria for definitive sign, determining a precise direction, and individual tactical movement/ awareness. Sign cutting tactics and search patterns are viable techniques, but these techniques should not replace the fundamentals that are paramount in establishing a solid skills foundation in the craft of tracking. Take the time at every opportunity to build that indicators file. You cannot catch anyone or anything by micro tracking, but the better you are at it, the less you will have to do it. This requires the use of all your senses and the ability to interpret what is going on around you.

As a Marine, I was aided in the execution of my duties by many handheld battery operated devices: communications, surveillance, target acquisition equipment, and long range ballistic capabilities. Combining these assets with the skills of visual tracking and advanced observation techniques is what will create the most capable 21st century American War fighters that have been 235 years in the making.

One last war story: after the battle for Najaf and our fight to clear its deadly cemetery, we were redeployed north in September to support operations near Fallujah. We were set up near Abu Ghraib prison, and we were to conduct counter IED patrols, respond to enemy sightings, as well as conduct raids on possible IED labs. During this time in 2004 we were rolling around in soft (unarmored) vehicles. We would roll down the roads going 5 miles an hour with our binoculars, looking for IEDs. I could see the application of tracking here as well because of the intelligence we would receive. We were told to look for freshly disturbed ground or ground that had variable temperatures when viewed with thermal devices. We remained very proactive in this area and had a significant effect on reducing the amount of friendly IED casualties. We did it effectively by using the tools God gave us: our eyes and attention to detail. We did not have electronic countermeasures on our vehicles back then, so the human senses were what kept us safe.

The funny thing about tracking is that it can consume you. You will find yourself always looking at the dirt. My son, Gabriel, can track decently for a seven-year-old, but I try to always make it fun for him. As he shows interest I will teach him more, and one day he will be far better at it than I am. Tracking is something that will call to a person. You cannot force it on them. If they are a tracker they will be drawn to it. Not everyone who has gone through a class is a tracker. He might be able to apply the practices of a tracker to his profession in some way, but after its discovery, if he is not completely consumed by it, he is not a tracker.

A tracker hungers for knowledge on the subject, and he tries new theories and practices his trade. This is what I have become. I became one through necessity, like the days in the desert where tracking helped me be a child again. Or, like the time spent in the deserts of the reform school where I could escape, or as a Marine to detect the presence of enemy IEDs. I even used it as a Marine Sniper to remain undetected by my enemy, and finally to keep my fellow warriors safe by showing them how to open their eyes to a world most people don't know exists. Tracking has called to me my whole life, and as I reflect, I can see that it has always been a part of who I am.

Earlier in the book I said the two most important things to accomplish while tracking is to know what to look for and know where to find it. It is my hope I have added to your ability to do that, and it helps you find the next track, wherever it may lead you.

For me there is only the traveling on paths that have heart, on any path that may have heart, and the only worthwhile challenge is to traverse its full length—and there I travel looking, looking breathlessly. —Carlos Casteneda, *The Teachings of Don Juan: A Yaqui Way of Knowledge*

About Freddy Osuna

Freddy Osuna began his tracking adventure as a young boy in the Sonoran Desert as the son of Freddy Osuna, Sr., a Yaqui Indian. There he found escape and great pleasure in discovering the secrets of the Desert Southwest. Before long he found himself and his brother as the foster children of a kind couple, Carmen and Octavio Pain—Octavio was a WWII U.S. Army Infantryman—but he continued his exploration of the wild, often tracking javelina, jack rabbit, and coyote.

As a young man, Freddy joined the United Sates Marine Corps as an infantryman. He served tours in the 2nd and 1st Marine Divisions, where he excelled as a student of military small unit tactics and deployed to Operation Iraqi Freedom 2 as a squad leader. Fighting in the streets and cemetery of Najaf Iraq, he witnessed firsthand the need for environmental awareness skills like tracking. Upon returning from Iraq, Freddy sought to return to combat a better-trained Marine, so he joined the Marine Scout Sniper Community, where he trained in modern survival and tracking skills. He began teaching tracking to snipers all over 1st Marine Division and advocating for the reinstitution of related field craft skills in the U.S. Marine Infantry and Scout Sniper professions.

Upon his honorable discharge from the U.S. Marines, Freddy taught hundreds of students from all the armed forces and federal, state, and local law enforcement agencies as a Combat Tracking Instructor at Ft. Huachuca, Arizona, and at locations all over the U.S. While at Ft. Huachuca, Freddy developed new programs as they applied to modern visual tracking skills and worked with the best police and military trackers in the world to hone his skills as a teacher and student of the craft.

In 2010 Freddy Osuna set off to create his own method of instructing tracking methods, and started Greenside Training, LLC, headquartered in Cochise County in Southeastern Arizona. As a trusted authority in the science of visual tracking, his life's passion—besides his wife

Amanda Osuna and sons Gabriel and Abel Osuna—is to advocate for the preservation and continuation in the teachings of the American craft of visual tracking.

To Learn More

To learn more on tracking and other outdoor skills, visit Freddy Osuna's website:

www.greensidetraining.com

Index

CPSIA information can be obtained at www.ICGtesting.com
Printed in the USA
LVIW01n0219301014
411205LV00002B/8

9 781935 354888